Most Delicious
Empanada Recipes

A little about empanadas.

An empanada is also called 'pastel' in Brazil and 'pate' in Haiti. You can find empanadas throughout Central- and South-America from Jamaica to Argentina. Even though the shapes and names aren't always the same and the ingredients vary, they always taste delicious! It's also nice to have a dish that is familiar to many different kinds of people. Another great thing about empanadas is that you can eat them in several ways: as breakfast, appetizers, dinner and even dessert. With just a bit of creativity, anybody can create innumerable flavor combinations. But these 50 recipes are the best ones we've tried! Try for yourselves and enjoy these delicious empanada recipes.

For updates about more awesome recipe books and free promotions like us on: www.facebook.com/OtherworldRecipes

CONTENTS

0. Empanada Dough 1

Fried Empanadas *2*

1. Yucca Empanadas 3
2. Cheese Empanadas 5
3. Sausage and Cheese Empanadas 6
4. Pork Empanadas 7
5. Colombian Beef and Potato Empanadas 9
6. Spicy Beef Empanadas 11
7. Venezuelan Chicken Empanadas 13
8. Chilean Seafood Empanadas 14
9. Pizza Empanadas 16
10. Ham and Cheese Empanadas 17
11. Plantain and Cheese Empanadas 19
12. Venezuelan Pabellon Empanadas 20
13. Shepherd's pie Empanadas 22
14. Argentine Beef Empanadas 23

Baked Empanadas *25*

15. Cheese, Spinach and Bacon Empanadas 26
16. Breakfast Empanadas 28
17. Buffalo Chicken Empanadas 30
18. Tuna Empanadas 31
19. BBQ Chicken Empanadas 33
20. Sausage, Potato and Cheese Empanada 35
21. Cream Cheese, Chicken and Jalapeños Empanadas 36

22. Shrimp and Cheese Empanada 38
23. Beef, Black beans and Corn Empanadas 40
24. Chicken Salad Empanada 41
25. Rice, Beans and Cheese Empanada 42
26. Turkey Empanada 43
27. Curry Chicken Empanada 44
28. Mashed Potatoes and Turkey Empanada 45

Vegetarian Empanadas *46*

29. Spinach and Cheese Empanada 47
30. Asparagus and Goat Cheese Empanada 49
31. Tomato and Cream Cheese Empanada 50
32. Potato and Peanut Empanada 52
33. Mushrooms Empanada 54
34. Quinoa and Goat Cheese Empanada 55
35. Green Plantain and Cheese Empanada 56
36. Plantain and Black Beans Empanada 57
37. Eggs and Potato Empanada 59
38. Eggplant Empanada 61

Sweet Empanadas *63*

39. Chocolate filled with Dulce de Leche Empanada 64
40. Banana Empanada 65
41. Apple and Cinnamon Empanada 66
42. Strawberry and Raspberry Empanada 68
43. Pineapple and Coconut Empanada 69
44. S'mores Empanada 70
45. Banana and Nutella Empanada 71
46. Blueberry and Chocolate Empanada 72
47. Strawberry and Cream Cheese Empanada 73

48. **Apricot and Cream Cheese Empanada**.....................................74
49. **Apricot, Banana and Ricotta Empanada**..................................75
50. **Nutella and Strawberry Empanada** 76

EMPANADA DOUGH

You can't make empanadas without empanada dough!

Yields: Dough for 12 empanadas

Ingredients:
1/3 cup ice water
1 large egg
2 1/4 cups unbleached all-purpose flour
Half cup cold unsalted butter (cut into ½ inch cubes)
1 ½ tsp salt
1 tablespoon distilled white vinegar

Method of Preparation
1. In a large bowl, sieve the flour with salt.
2. Knead in the butter with your hands until the mixture looks crumbly.
3. In a smaller bowl beat the egg together with vinegar and water.
4. To flour mixture, add the egg mixture while stirring with fork until barely incorporated. Don't mix too much.
5. Put the mixture onto a floured surface
6. Knead with your hand's heel twice, just enough to make it into a quick dough.
7. Shape the dough into a flat rectangle and wrap it in plastic.
8. Let the dough chill for at least an hour.
9. Split the dough up into 12 equal pieces and turn the pieces into 12 balls.
10. With a lightly floured rolling pin, roll 1 ball out on a floured surface into a 5 inch disc (about 1/8 inch thick). Make sure to keep the rest covered with a damp towel while doing this
11. Do the same with the rest and keep the ones that are done also covered.
12. That's it, you can now use them to create empanadas

Fried Empanadas

YUCCA EMPANADAS

Most of the empanadas are made with flour or cornmeal but these ones are made out of yucca. One of the best health benefits of this root is that it has antioxidant properties; this can help to prevent diseases like some of the cardiovascular ones. Another good thing about yucca is that it eases diabetes symptoms and helps to have favorable cholesterol levels.

Yields: Makes 18 empanadas.

Ingredients:
1 pound frozen peeled yucca
2 tbsp extra-virgin olive oil
A pinch of salt
1 small red onion, chopped
1 red bell pepper, finely diced
2 garlic cloves, minced
¼ tsp ground turmeric
½ tsp smoked sweet paprika
½ tsp ground cumin
1 tsp crushed red pepper
2 tbsp chopped golden raisins
2 scallions, minced
2 tbsp red wine vinegar
½ cup Brazil nuts
4 ounces fresh mozzarella, diced
Vegetable oil, for deep-frying

Method of Preparation:
1. In a saucepan, cover the yucca with water and boil it over around 27 minutes. Drain and put it back in the pan, shake over heat to dry

it out (10-15 seconds). Pass it through a ricer and add a pinch of salt. Start kneading the yucca to form dough, cover it with plastic wrap and let cool.

2. In a large pan, heat the olive oil, onion, red bell pepper and garlic, cook until softened. Add the turmeric, cumin, paprika and red pepper and cook, stirring for 1 minute. Add the raisins, scallions and vinegar and cook until the vinegar has been absorbed, then let cool.

3. Toast the Brazil nuts in the oven for 5 minutes, and then chop. (350°)

4. Stir the nuts and mozzarella cheese into the onion mixture.

5. Oil your hands and take a tbsp of yucca dough, form a 2 ½ -inch round, add a tsp of the filling and close the dough

6. In a saucepan, heat vegetable oil to 375°

7. Fry the empanadas until golden and crisp.

CHEESE EMPANADAS

You have to do some appetizers but nothing comes to mind. What about some cheese empanadas? They are easy and delicious. It's true that you can let your creativity go and make thousands of ingredients combinations but I'm pretty sure that almost everyone loves cheese empanadas at any time!

Yields: 40 mini empanadas

Ingredients:
3 cups cornmeal
A pinch of salt
12 oz mozzarella cheese (whatever cheese you want)
Oil, for deep frying

Method of Preparation:
1. Place the cornmeal into a bowl, add a pinch of salt and then around 2- 2 ½ cups of water, knead until form a dough.
2. Take a tbsp of dough and put it on a piece of plastic wrap
3. Make a 4 inch circle of dough
4. Add the cheese (any shape, it's going to melt anyways)
5. Fold the circle in half, making a moon shape
6. Close it with a fork
7. In a saucepan, heat the oil to 375°
8. Fry the empanadas until golden and crisp.

Sausage and Cheese Empanadas

Sausages are just fantastic, they come in several ways and flavors ¡The spicy ones are the best for me! When you combine crispy dough with sausages and melted cheese, you just want to eat like thousands of them. Make big empanadas for a delicious breakfast or prepare little ones to accompany another dish.

Yields: 12 empanadas

Ingredients:
12 empanadas discs for frying
1 tbsp butter
½ white onion, diced
1 lb sausages (your favorite kind)
12 oz mozzarella or Oaxaca cheese
Oil, for deep frying

Method of Preparation:
1. Take a pan and put some butter over low heat. Add the onions and cook them for about 5 minutes.
2. Cut the sausages in little pieces and add them into the pan with onions. Cook until the sausages are done and then let it cool down.
3. Take one of the empanada discs; add some cheese and sausages in the center. Fold it in a moon shape and seal it with a fork
4. In a frying pan, heat the oil to 375°
5. Fry the empanadas until golden and crisp on each side.

PORK EMPANADAS

This is one of those recipes that are easy, rich in nutrients and especially tasty. Many people have a bad concept about pork. The truth is that pork is a great source of protein, vitamins and minerals as iron, B1, B6, B12 and zinc. Not too bad, right? If you combine that with some veggies, it can create an excellent mix to serve a nice lunch or dinner.

Yields: 12 empanadas

Ingredients:
2 tbsp vegetable oil
2 cloves garlic, minced
1 tomato, diced
1 onion, diced
1 carrot, diced
1 lb pork, minced
1 pork stock cube
A pinch of salt
½ cup peas
1 large potato, diced
1 tsp sugar
1/8 cup water

For the dough:
3 cups plain flour
½ tsp baking powder
½ tsp salt
8.8 oz butter, cubed
¼ cup water
1 egg

Method of Preparation:

1. Start cooking the onion, tomato, pork and pork cube. Stir the mixture and add salt, potato and water. Keep stirring for about 5 minutes, you'll see the pork almost done.
2. Add the carrot, and keep cooking the mix around 8 minutes, finally add peas and sugar, keep it over heat for two more minutes and then let it cool down.
3. It's time to make the pastry. Combine flour, baking powder salt and butter.
4. Begin to rub the butter with the dry ingredients until get a crumbly mixture.
5. Add water and egg.
6. Knead until get a soft dough
7. Make dough circles, add the filling in the middle and close it in a moon shape.
8. Heat the vegetable oil in a pan and cook the empanadas until golden and crisp

Colombian Beef and Potato Empanadas

In some countries, empanadas are baked but in Colombia most of their empanadas are fried, fried, fried. If you visit Colombia, or maybe meet some Colombians, they are going to tell you how much they love empanadas; it's like a part of their life. Most of them use empanadas for breakfast or brunch because it's not as heavy as other Colombian dishes but it's good enough to be a nice meal for the morning.

Yields: 12 empanadas

Ingredients:
2 tbsp olive oil
2 cloves garlic, minced
½ tsp cumin
1 tomato, chopped
1 small onion, chopped
¼ cup cilantro leaves, chopped
1 pound skirt steak, striped
3 beef bouillon cubes
½ pound potato
A pinch of salt
2 tsp sugar
3 cups precooked cornmeal
Vegetable oil, for frying

Method of Preparation:
1. Heat the oil in a large pot and start adding: tomato, garlic, onion, salt, cumin, and cilantro. Stir until the onion becomes soft. This is going to last 10-12 minutes.
2. In a separate bowl, mix beef bouillon cubes and steak stripes, cover the meat with water and bring it to boil.

3. After about an hour, add the potatoes to the pot with the beef and let it cook until both are done.
4. Prepare the dough. Mix the precooked cornmeal with 2 cups of water and sugar (if you rather your empanadas saltier, skip the sugar).
5. Knead until soft.
6. Separate the dough into 12 balls and make them flat.
7. Add the beef with potatoes and the first mixture in the middle of the dough.
8. Fold the circle in half, making a moon shape, seal the dough with a fork or your fingers.
9. Preheat the vegetable oil and start frying the empanadas until golden.

SPICY BEEF EMPANADAS

There are some people that love to eat spicy food. If you visit Mexico you'll see fruits with spicy sauce, spicy powders for popcorns, awesome, right? Well, spicy food is everywhere and it's an exotic taste that brings life in different dishes. These spicy beef empanadas are perfect for an appetizer, prepare them for your next party and everyone is going to ask you for the recipe.

Yields: 20 empanadas

Ingredients:
20 empanadas discs for frying
2 lbs ground beef
2 tbsp olive oil
3 cloves garlic, minced
1 sweet pepper, chopped
5 tbsp tomato paste
Your favorite hot sauce
A pinch of onion powder
A pinch of oregano
Crushed red pepper flakes
Salt and pepper to taste
2 tbsp water
Vegetable oil, for frying

Method of Preparation:
1. Preheat a pot and start seasoning the vegetables: garlic, pepper, salt, oregano, and onions with the olive oil.
2. When you see the veggies becoming toasty, add the ground beef.
3. You have to season the meat also, add all the spices that you want, remember it has to be really rich in taste.

4. Add the tomato paste and mix it well with the beef.
5. Finally, add hot sauce! A bit of a time, keep in mind that then you can't take off the sauce, so be careful.
6. Now it's time to assemble the empanadas. Take one of the discs and put some of the spicy beef in the middle. Close it in half and that's all.
7. Fry them in hot vegetable oil until golden and crisp.

Venezuelan Chicken Empanadas

Empanadas are one of the most famous plates in Venezuela. You can find them almost in every corner because are the second favorite thing for breakfast, after arepas. There, empanadas are cheap and extra delicious; also they have different dips to eat with them. Here's a simple recipe to make chicken empanadas, Venezuelan style.

Yields: 4 empanadas

Ingredients:
1 cup precooked cornmeal
½ cup water
½ tsp salt
½ pound chicken breast
1 tomato, diced
1 onion, diced
Vegetable oil, for frying

Method of Preparation:
1. Boil the chicken with a pinch of salt. After cooked, cut it in stripes and put it into a pan with the tomato and onion. Let it cool down.
2. Prepare the dough with the cornmeal, water and salt. If you want the dough to be a bit sweeter, add around a tsp of sugar.
3. Knead until soft.
4. Divide the dough in four and make circles with each part.
5. Make it flat and put the chicken in the middle of the circle. Close it in half and seal it with a fork.
6. Heat the vegetable oil in a pan and fry the empanadas, be careful.
7. Enjoy!

Chilean Seafood Empanadas

Chileans eat a lot of seafood, and they make big empanadas, large enough for a meal. So, if you combine those two you end with a seafood empanada ready for lunch. This recipe is with mussels, they're a great source of vitamin B12, zinc and protein.

Yields: 12 empanadas

Ingredients:
2lbs mussels
1 cup water
2 onions, chopped
A pinch of pepper
Vegetable oil, for frying

For the dough
5.3 oz plain flour
5.3 oz cornstarch
2.5 oz butter, melted
A pinch of salt

Method of Preparation:
1. Clean the mussels, put them in a pot, add water and boil them for two minutes.
2. Add the onions and keep cooking for another two minutes.
3. Spice it up with a pinch of pepper.
4. Let it cool down to assemble the empanadas.
5. Now let's do the dough, mix all the dry ingredients and then add the melted butter. The butter must be cold.
6. Knead until get soft dough.
7. Make 12 balls, flat them with a roller.

8. Put some of the mussels in the middle and seal it in a half moon shape.
9. Heat the vegetable oil and fry the empanadas for about two minutes or until golden.

Pizza Empanadas

Who doesn't like pizza? For real. Pizza is one of the most popular foods worldwide. You can find it almost everywhere. Now think about this, pizza + empanadas, it sounds perfect, right? This recipe is the ideal for a party meal or just for a Sunday brunch. If you like pizza, you'll love these empanadas.

Yields: 30 empanadas

Ingredients:
30 won ton wrappers
3 cups pizza sauce
A pinch of pepper
10 oz mozzarella cheese
8 oz pepperoni
Vegetable oil, for frying

Method of Preparation:
1. In a pot, mix the pizza sauce with the pepper to give it more flavor.
2. Put some of the mozzarella cheese, pizza sauce and a pepperoni in the middle of each won ton wrapper.
3. Seal the won ton wrappers with a fork in a half moon shape.
4. If you want, you can add some corn.
5. Heat the vegetable oil in a pan.
6. Start frying the little empanadas until crisp, about 30-45 seconds.

Ham and Cheese Empanadas

Ham and Cheese is the perfect combination for breakfast. If you want to make something easy, yet yummy, this is the perfect recipe. You don't need a lot of ingredients and you can always use different kind of cheese leftovers to make it extra delicious!

Yields: 15 empanadas

Ingredients:
1 pound cheese
½ pound ham, diced
A pinch of pepper
Vegetable oil, for frying

For the dough:
4 cups all-purpose flour
¼ cup water
2 eggs, beaten
3 tbsp butter
2 tsp baking powder
1 tsp salt

Method of Preparation:
1. Combine the cheese with the ham and spice it with some pepper.
2. For the dough, mix all the dry ingredients.
3. Then, add the butter, eggs and water.
4. Knead and create soft dough.
5. Let it rest for about 5 minutes.
6. Divide the dough in 15 balls. Flat the balls with a roller.
7. Add a tbsp of the filling in the middle of each circle.
8. Fold the dough making a half moon shape.

9. Dip your fingers in water and seal the border, after do the same but with a fork.
10. Fry them with a lot of vegetable oil.

PLANTAIN AND CHEESE EMPANADAS

Plantains are awesome because you can make hundreds of recipes with them. They can be boiled, steamed, baked, grilled or…fried! This recipe calls for fried yummy plantains. If you use green plantains the taste is going to be more neutral, but if you cook with a really yellow plantain, it'll taste sweeter and that one is better for this so you'll have the mix of sweet and salty. Also, plantains are a great source of vitamin C!

Yields: 12 empanadas

Ingredients:
2 large yellow plantains
12 oz of cheese (mozzarella works fine with this recipe)
Vegetable oil, for frying

For the dough
3 cups cornmeal
1 cup water
A pinch of salt

Method of Preparation:
1. Cut the plantains in little circles.
2. Fry the plantains with plenty vegetable oil, until browned. Then let them cooled in absorbent paper.
3. For the dough, mix the dry ingredients and then add water.
4. Knead until get soft dough.
5. Make 12 balls; flat them with a roller or your hands.
6. Put some of the cheese and three-five plantains in the middle of the dough; seal it in a half moon shape.
7. Heat the vegetable oil and fry the empanadas until golden.

Venezuelan Pabellon Empanadas

What is Pabellon? The Pabellon criollo is a traditional Venezuelan dish. It contains white rice, black beans, slices of flank steak and tajadas (yellow plantain, fried). Sounds good, don't you think? Now picture all those ingredients inside a crispy empanada.

Yields: 12 empanadas

Ingredients:
1 lb flank steak
1 beef cube
3 cloves garlic
2 onions, chopped
2 tbsp butter
2 tomatoes, diced
A pinch of salt
1 ½ cup rice
1 ½ cup black beans
2 yellow plantains, fried
Vegetable oil, for frying

For the dough:
3 cup precooked cornmeal
1 cup water
½ tsp salt

Method of Preparation:
1. Boil the flank steak with the beef cup and salt. After about 2 hours, the meat is going to be tender. You'll have to slice it really thin, almost like hair.
2. In a pan, add the garlic, tomato, onions and the flank. If you want to spice it up a little bit, add some pepper.

3. After the meat is done, it's time to mix it up with the black beans and the rice. If you want to put them separate it's ok too.
4. For the empanada dough, mix all the dry ingredients first and then add water.
5. Knead the dough until soft.
6. Make dough circles and put a bit of each filling in the middle of the dough (meat, rice, black beans and plantains)
7. Close the dough in a half moon shape.
8. Fry them very well with vegetable oil, until crisp.

SHEPHERD'S PIE EMPANADAS

This is a traditional British dish. It's a pie made with lamb, mashed potatoes, carrots, peas and cheese. Usually people cook a lot of pie for a dinner or lunch but, what are you going to do with the leftovers? Yes, that's right, empanadas! One of the best things about empanadas is that you can use almost every leftover to make a new tasty meal.

Yields: 12 empanadas

Ingredients:
12 empanadas discs for frying
1 lbs lamb
2 cups mashed potato
8oz cheese
1 tbs butter
A pinch of pepper
1 carrot, diced
1 cup peas
Vegetable oil, for frying

Method of Preparation:
1. If you don't have shepherd's pie leftovers, just fill the empanada with the ingredients, separated.
2. First, cook the lamb in your favorite way. The mashed potato can be spiced with some pepper and butter, mix the carrots and peas with it.
3. Fill each empanada disc with lamb, mashed potato and cheese.
4. Seal the discs in a half moon shape.
5. Fry each disc in vegetable oil; wait for them to be golden on each side.

Argentine Beef Empanadas

This recipe is perfect for a lunch. If you want to make something different and heavy enough for a lunch, this is the one. Some of them add eggs to these empanadas, but there's also a version without eggs. Interesting fact: Argentina has a National Empanada Festival; awesome, right?

Yields: 12 empanadas

Ingredients:
1 lb ground beef
½ cup onions, chopped
½ cup olives
4 boiled eggs, sliced
3 tomatoes, diced
2 oz bacon, chopped
3 cloves garlic
3 tbsp butter
¼ tsp cumin
Vegetable oil, for frying

For the dough:
4 cups all-purpose flour
¼ cup water
2 eggs, beaten
3 tbsp butter
2 tsp baking powder
1 tsp salt

Method of Preparation:
1. In a pan, cook the butter, bacon, garlic and onions. After a couple of minutes, add the ground beef.

23

2. Mix well and start adding the spices.
3. Now include the tomatoes and the olives in the mixture. Cook over low heat until the beef is done, let it cool down.
4. Prepare the dough, mix all the dry ingredients.
5. Add butter, eggs and water.
6. Knead until create soft dough.
7. Let it rest for about 5 minutes.
8. Divide the dough in 12 balls. Flat the balls with a roller.
9. Add a tbsp of the filling in the middle of each circle.
10. Fold the dough making a half moon shape.
11. Dip your fingers in water and seal the border.
12. Fry them with a lot of vegetable oil.

<u>Baked Empanadas</u>

Cheese, Spinach and Bacon Empanadas

Everything is better when you add some bacon. These empanadas are healthier than the fried version; also they have spinach, a veggie that is really low in calories and full of nutrients like vitamin A and C.

Yields: 12 empanadas

Ingredients:
1 tbsp butter
2 cloves garlic, minced
8 oz fresh spinach, washed
1 cup ricotta cheese
8 oz white cheese
A pinch of salt
A pinch of pepper

For the dough:
1 cup water
¾ cup butter
3 cup flour
A pinch of salt

Method of Preparation:
1. Heat the butter in a pan and start adding the garlic, after a couple of minutes you are going to start smelling the garlic, then, add the spinach.
2. Put the ricotta and mozzarella cheese; spice it up with salt and pepper.
3. Prepare the dough, heat water and butter until the butter is totally melted.
4. In a bowl, add the flour and salt; make a hole in the middle and start adding the liquid while kneading a bit.

26

5. You are going to get wet dough, wrap it in plastic and refrigerate for at least 3 hours.
6. Preheat the oven 375°.
7. Divide the dough in 12 balls.
8. Roll the dough in a circle shape, add about a tbsp of the filling in the middle and then close the dough in a half moon shape.
9. Put them on a baking sheet and bake for 25 minutes.

BREAKFAST EMPANADAS

Eggs and sausages, that's breakfast. These empanadas are perfect for a big breakfast or brunch. You can make them fried too but baked is a bit healthier and really yummy. Choose your favorite type of sausage as there is a big list of different kinds.

Yields: 14 empanadas

Ingredients:
½ pound sausages
1 tsp vegetable oil
½ large onion
6 eggs, beaten
A pinch of salt
¼ cup cheese

For the dough:
1 cup water
6 oz butter
3 cups flour
A pinch of salt

Method of Preparation:
1. Heat the oil and cook the sausages in a pan.
2. When the sausages are almost ready, add the onion, and cook until they become translucent.
3. Finally, add the eggs, salt and cheese, stir until everything is done.
4. For the dough, Take a pan and heat water and butter until the butter is totally melted.
5. In a bowl, add the flour and salt; make a hole in the middle and start adding the liquid while kneading.

6. Going to get wet dough, wrap it in plastic and refrigerate from 2 to 3 hours before use.
7. Separate 14 pieces of dough and roll them in a circular shape.
8. Add the filling in the middle of dough and enclose it in half.
9. Press the border with your fingers.
10. Preheat the oven 400°.
11. Cook the empanadas for 20-25 minutes.

Buffalo Chicken Empanadas

Party food! These mini empanadas are perfect for any kind of celebration. These are one of those delicious foods that everybody wants to eat in a meeting, and they don't want to eat just one… Serve them with different types of sauces and I'm sure the guests are going to love you.

Yields: 48 mini empanadas

Ingredients:
8 oz cream cheese
12 oz canned chicken, drained
1 cup cheddar cheese
¼ cup buffalo sauce
1 egg, beaten
48 mini empanada discs

Method of Preparation:
1. Preheat oven to 400°
2. Take a bowl and mix chicken, cream cheese, cheddar cheese and buffalo sauce.
3. Take one of the empanada discs and put about ½ tbsp of filling in the middle of each one.
4. Fold the disc in half and, with a fork, push the borders so the filling does not comes out while baking.
5. Bake the empanadas for 15 minutes or until golden.

Tuna Empanadas

Tuna is full of protein, is good for preventing strokes, heart diseases and obesity. It contains vitamin B and Omega-3, sounds really well for your health, right? This is why you have to try these empanadas.

Yields: 8 empanadas

Ingredients:
1 can tuna
3 tbsp peeled tomatoes
¼ cup onions, chopped
A pinch of salt
A pinch of pepper
2 cloves garlic, mashed

For the dough:
2 cups all-purpose flour
1/3 cup butter
2 eggs
2 tbsp water
2 tsp baking powder
1 egg yolk

Method of Preparation:
1. For the dough, mix all the dry ingredients in a large bowl.
2. Make a hole in the middle of the bowl and add the butter in little cubes, start mixing it with the flour.
3. Beat the eggs a bit and add them in the mix, add the water. Stir until get soft dough.
4. Let it rest for 5 minutes.
5. Preheat the oven to 300°.

6. For the tuna filling, in a pan, mix the tuna with all the other ingredients.
7. If you want to spice it more, add more than a pinch of salt and pepper.
8. Take a piece of dough; roll it until have a circular flat shape.
9. Add a tbsp of tuna filling inside each dough circle.
10. Close it in a half moon shape.
11. Bake for 15 minutes.

BBQ Chicken Empanadas

Do you have chicken leftovers? You need a recipe to take advantage of it? What about BBQ Chicken empanadas for dinner? Everybody is going to say yes to this question.

Yields: 6 empanadas

Ingredients:
2 cups shredded chicken
1 cup BBQ sauce
½ cup onions
1 cup cheese

For the dough:
1 ½ cup all purpose flour
6 tbsp butter, chilled
A pinch of salt
2 tbsp water

Method of Preparation:
1. Cook the onions a bit in a pan.
2. Then, in a pot, add the onions, chicken, BBQ sauce and part of the cheese (like half a cup), set aside.
3. Prepare the dough; mix all the dry ingredients in a large bowl.
4. Make a hole in the middle of the bowl and add the chilled butter, start mixing it with the flour.
5. Add the water to the dough until get a soft mixture.
6. Let the dough rest for 10 minutes at least.
7. Divide the dough into 6 pieces.
8. Make a flat circle with each dough piece.
9. Add a tbsp of filling in the middle of each dough circle, fold it in

half and close it making pressure with your fingers in the border. Put some of the cheese on top after the empanada is closed.

10. Preheat the oven to 350°.
11. Bake the empanadas for 25 minutes, until golden and fluffy.

Sausage, Potato and Cheese Empanada

If you want to make a quick lunch, take some sausages, potatoes, and make a bunch of empanadas. This is perfect for a take-to-go lunch, maybe if you have to go to school or work. Also, if you want to make a real complete lunch in an empanada, add some veggies.

Yields: 16 empanadas

Ingredients:
8 large sausages
3 potatoes, boiled and sliced
2 cups cheddar cheese
A pinch of salt
A pinch of pepper
16 empanada discs

Method of Preparation:
1. Cook the sausages and cut them in little pieces.
2. In a pan, mix the sausages, potatoes, salt, pepper and cheese; Stir until the cheese is melted.
3. Preheat the oven to 400°
4. Take each empanada disc and put a 1-2 tbsp of the filling in the middle.
5. Close the disc in a half and press the borders with a fork.
6. Bake for 15 minutes or until golden.

CREAM CHEESE, CHICKEN AND JALAPEÑOS EMPANADAS

Do you know jalapeño poppers? Well, these are jalapeños empanadas! This is an easy, tasty and useful recipe. Make them for parties, lunch, snacks, whatever you want. Did you know that the jalapeños are a great source of vitamin C?

Yields: 30 empanadas

Ingredients:
8 oz cream cheese
2 cups cooked shredded chicken
1 ½ cups cheddar cheese
3 oz jalapeños, diced
1 egg, beaten
A pinch of salt
A pinch of pepper

For the dough:
4 cups all-purpose flour
3/4 cup butter
1 ¼ cups water
2 tsp baking powder
A pinch of salt

Method of Preparation:
1. In a pot, melt the cream cheese and then add the chicken, salt, pepper, jalapeños and cheddar cheese.
2. In a little bowl, beat the egg and hold it there.
3. For the dough, mix all the dry ingredients and then add the butter, after everything is well mixed (dry ingredients + butter), start pouring water into the mixture. Knead it until it becomes soft dough.

36

4. Take a little piece of dough and roll it until get a flat circle.
5. Add a tbsp of the filling in each circle.
6. Fold the dough in half and seal it with a fork.
7. Preheat the oven to 400°
8. Before baking the empanadas, brush them with the egg on the top, this is going to make them browner.
9. Bake the empanadas for 15-18 minutes.

SHRIMP AND CHEESE EMPANADA

Facts about shrimps: an average shrimp has 10 legs; they come in various colors like white, pink, red and some really weird ones like blue and tigers; May 9th is National Shrimp Day. So, every May 9th we should bake some shrimp and cheese empanadas, here is the recipe.

Yields: 16 empanadas

Ingredients:
2 tbsp olive oil
½ cup onions, chopped
2 cloves garlic, mashed
1 lb shrimp, peeled, deveined and chopped.
4 tomatoes
A pinch of salt
1 cup mozzarella cheese, grated
1 tbsp milk
1 egg, beaten
16 empanada discs

Method of Preparation:
1. Put the olive oil in skillet over medium heat, add the onions and garlic, stir for about 5 minutes.
2. Incorporate the shrimps into the skillet, cook until the shrimps turn pinkish.
3. Add tomatoes, salt and garlic.
4. Keep cooking until everything is done and put aside to let the filling cold down.
5. Take each empanada disc and put a big tbsp of filling in the middle of each circle.
6. Fold the discs in half and close it with a fork

7. Preheat the oven to 375°
8. Beat the egg with the milk and brush that mixture over the empanadas
9. Bake the empanadas for 20-25 minutes or until golden.

Beef, Black beans and Corn Empanadas

Corn is in more foods that we imagine, you can find it inside cereal, peanut butter, some snacks and even soda. It has a lot of vitamins and amino acids. So, what about making baked empanadas with some corn? This recipe mix corn, beef and healthy black beans.

Yields: 10 empanadas

Ingredients:
1 lb ground beef
A pinch of salt
A pinch of pepper
1 tbsp olive oil
2 onions, chopped
6 cloves garlic, minced
1/2 cup frozen corn kernels
1/2 cup canned black beans, rinsed
1/2 cup shredded cheese
10 empanada discs

Method of Preparation:
1. Heat the olive oil in a saucepan and sauté the garlic and onions.
2. Add the corn and black beans into the pan.
3. After 5 minutes over medium heat, add the beef.
4. Season the beef with a pinch of salt and pepper.
5. Let the mixture cool down.
6. Preheat the oven to 375°
7. Take each empanada disc and put a tbsp of filling in the middle (maybe a bit more)
8. Close the disc in a half moon shape.
9. Bake for 30 minutes.

CHICKEN SALAD EMPANADA

What to do with chicken leftovers; or more specific, chicken salad leftovers. Empanadas of course! Remember that you can always take advantage of that food that you keep saving in little packaging into the fridge. Take off all of them and prepare empanadas.

Yields: 8 empanadas

Ingredients:
2 cups chicken, shredded and cooked
1/2 cup mayonnaise
1/3 cup toasted pecans, chopped
1/4 cup celery, chopped
2 tbsp lemon juice
3/4 tsp salt
1/4 tsp black pepper
8 refrigerated jumbo biscuits

Method of Preparation:
1. Preheat the oven to 350°
2. In a pan, over low heat, stir together the chicken, mayo, celery, lemon, pecans, salt and pepper for about 1 minute.
3. Roll the biscuits into 6 inches circles.
4. Put 2 tbsp of filling into each circle.
5. Fold the biscuits in half and seal it pressing the borders with a fork.
6. Bake for 25 minutes or until golden.

RICE, BEANS AND CHEESE EMPANADA

When you read rice, beans and cheese, one of the very first things that come into your mind is a burrito, or not? This empanada is perfect to eat with hot sauce and some guacamole.

Yields: 8 empanadas

Ingredients:
10 empanada discs
1 cup rice, cooked
1 cup refried beans (your favorite)
2 cup cheese, shredded
½ cup tomato salsa

Method of Preparation:
1. In a bowl, mix really well all the ingredients.
2. Put a full tbsp of the filling into each empanada disc.
3. Fold over the disc and seal it with a fork or your fingers.
4. Preheat the oven to 400°
5. Bake the empanadas for 25 minutes.
6. Serve with hot sauce and guacamole.

Turkey Empanada

These empanadas are perfect for the breakfast after holidays, yes; turkey leftovers are the main ingredient. Be creative, put some corn or cheese, and serve them with some garlic or cheddar cheese sauce.

Yields: 12 empanadas

Ingredients:
12 empanadas discs
2 tbsp butter
½ onion, sliced
½ bell pepper, sliced
3 cloves garlic, crushed
2 tomatoes, diced
1 tsp ground cumin
2 cups turkey, shredded
2 tbsp turkey gravy (if you have some leftovers)
½ tbsp oregano
A pinch of salt

Method of Preparation:
1. In a pan, melt the butter.
2. Add the onions, tomatoes, bell pepper, garlic, oregano and cumin.
3. Stir while cooking over medium heat around 12 minutes.
4. Mix in the shredded turkey and gravy; keep stirring.
5. Add one tbsp of the turkey mixture on to the center of each dough disc.
6. Fold the empanada disc and seal the edges with a fork.
7. Preheat the oven to 400°.
8. Bake for 25 minutes or until golden.

CURRY CHICKEN EMPANADA

It's time to make something a little more exotic. Some people are a little bit scared of cooking with curry but actually it's not that difficult. This recipe is really simple and goes really well with baked empanadas. Do something different for tonight's dinner.

Yields: 12 empanadas

Ingredients:
3 tbsp olive oil
2 lb ground chicken
2 onions, diced
2 tbsp ginger, grated
4 cloves garlic, minced
½ tsp cumin
1 tsp salt
4 tbsp curry powder
1 cup petit peas

Method of Preparation:
1. In a pan, heat the oil on medium heat.
2. Sauté the, garlic and onions for about 3 minutes.
3. Add curry powder, salt and cumin first to bring out the flavors.
4. Then add the ground chicken.
5. After the chicken is done, add the petit peas and carrots. Combine and set aside.
6. Place a tbsp of filling in the center of each empanada wrapper.
7. Fold in half and seal the edge with a fork.
8. Preheat the oven to 400°.
9. Bake for 20-25 minutes.

Mashed Potatoes and Turkey Empanada

These are what I call "Thanksgiving Empanadas". You can make some of the empanadas with homemade gravy or make a cranberry sauce to eat with these. Does not sounds delicious to you? Make them mini for holiday's parties!

Yields: 12 empanadas

Ingredients:
4 cups cooked turkey, chopped
3 cups mashed potatoes
1/4 tsp cumin
A pinch of salt
A pinch of pepper
12 empanada discs

Method of Preparation:
1. Mix together the turkey, mashed potatoes and cumin. Add salt and pepper.
2. Preheat the oven to 450°.
3. Put a tbsp into each empanada disc.
4. Fold the disc in half and close the dough with your fingers or a fork.
5. Bake for 15 minutes or until golden.
6. Don't over bake because they'd be too dry.

<u>Vegetarian Empanadas</u>

Spinach and Cheese Empanada

Popeye's favorite food! These vegetarian empanadas are a great option for someone that wants something yummy without any kind of meat. Try some of these for lunch and enjoy a healthy meal. Remember that spinach is a fabulous source of vitamins and minerals.

Yields: 12 empanadas

Ingredients:
4 tbsp olive oil
3 cloves garlic, minced
8 oz fresh spinach
1 cup ricotta cheese
8 oz mozzarella cheese, shredded.
2 tbsp parmesan cheese, grated
A pinch of salt
A pinch of pepper

For the dough:
1 cup water
3/4 cup butter
2 3/4 cups flour
2 tsp salt

Method of Preparation:
1. Heat the olive oil in a pan over medium high heat.
2. Add the minced garlic
3. Add the spinach and sauté until all the greens are faded.
4. Remove from the pan and put it into a bowl.
5. Stir the ricotta cheese, mozzarella and parmesan.
6. Move the mixture until is still hot.

7. Flavor it with salt and pepper.
8. For the dough, heat the water and butter until butter has melted.
9. Combine dry ingredients in a bowl and make a hole in the center.
10. Pour the warm liquid in and stir.
11. Knead until get soft dough and let it rest for at least 2 hours.
12. Preheat the oven to 375°.
13. Separate 12 dough balls.
14. Roll the dough balls until flat circle.
15. Put a tbsp of spinach filling in middle of each circle.
16. Seal the dough folding it in half and pressuring the edges with your fingers.
17. Bake for 30 minutes.

Asparagus and Goat Cheese Empanada

Goat cheese is a really good option for cheese lovers. It contains a lot of healthy benefits that maybe you don't know, here are some of them: goat cheese is high in protein, helps you to boost the metabolism, it's really low in calories and fat. So, this vegetarian recipe is perfect.

Yields: 12 empanadas

Ingredients:
2 tbsp butter
½ cup onions, diced
½ lb of asparagus
1 cup green peas
4 oz goat cheese, crumbled
A pinch of salt
A pinch of pepper
12 empanada discs
1 egg, beaten

Method of Preparation:
1. In a pan, melt the butter over medium heat.
2. Add the onions and cook for about 3 minutes.
3. Then, add the asparagus and cook for another 4-5 minutes.
4. Add the peas and cook for another couple of minutes.
5. Add salt and pepper.
6. Take each of the empanada discs and fill them with the asparagus mixture.
7. Close the dough in horn shape, seal it with a fork.
8. Preheat the oven to 400°
9. Before baking, brush over the empanadas with the egg.
10. Bake for 25 minutes or a bit more, wait until gets gold.

TOMATO AND CREAM CHEESE EMPANADA

This combination is soft, healthy, and yummy. It's perfect for snacking in a meeting. Tomatoes are low in calories, around 15 calories per each 100g. They contain vitamin A, vitamin C, and many other nutrients like calcium, iron and zinc.

Yields: 12 empanadas

Ingredients:
4 tomatoes, diced
1 onion, shredded
1 tbsp olive oil
A pinch of pepper
A pinch of salt
8 oz cream cheese

For the dough:
 2 cup flour
3/4 cup butter
½ cup water
1 egg
2 tsp salt

Method of Preparation:
1. In a pan, put in the onions over medium heat.
2. Add tomatoes, salt and pepper and cook for about 5 minutes.
3. Heat the oven to 350°
4. For the dough, mix all dry ingredients, add the egg and then start kneading a bit.
5. Let the dough rest for 10 minutes before bake it.
6. Roll the dough and cut out circles shapes.

7. Put a tbsp of filling and a tsp of cream cheese into each circle.
8. Seal the dough folding it in half and pressing the border with a fork.
9. Bake for 30 minutes.

POTATO AND PEANUT EMPANADA

These empanadas are typical in Colombia. There' they call them "Pipián empanada". This is an empanada full of peanuts and potato that they usually prepare for breakfast or snacking.

Yields: 10 empanadas

Ingredients:
1 egg, cooked and chopped
3 potatoes, smashed
1 cup roasted peanuts, chopped
A pinch of salt
A pinch of pepper
2 tbsp oil
2 tomatoes, chopped
1/4 cup onion, chopped
1 clove garlic, minced
2 tbsp cilantro, chopped

For the dough:
11/4 cup water
1 cup butter
3 cups flour
2 tsp salt

Method of Preparation:
1. Take a skillet and heat the oil.
2. Add the onion and cook for about 5 minutes.
3. Add the tomatoes, garlic, cilantro, salt and black pepper. Cook for about 12 minutes.
4. Add the diced and cooked potatoes and mix.

5. For the dough, first heat the water and butter until everything is combine.
6. Mix dry ingredients in a bowl and make a hole in the center.
7. Add the buttery liquid in and stir.
8. Knead until get soft dough and let it rest for at least 2-3 hours.
9. Preheat the oven to 375°.
10. Roll the dough until flat and cut, with a glass or cookie cutter, 10 big circles.
11. Put a tbsp of the potato filling in middle of each circle.
12. Seal the dough folding it in half and pressuring the border with your fingers.
13. Bake for 30 minutes.

MUSHROOMS EMPANADA

Empanadas are the best option to make for appetizers. You can make them in petit style and everybody is going to love them. These vegetarian empanadas are perfect to serve with some dipping sauces like a fresh tomato sauce with some herbs.

Yields: 25 mini empanadas

Ingredients:
2 tbsp butter
3 cups mushrooms, sliced
¼ cup raisins
2 tsp balsamic vinegar
1 cup cheese, grated
1 egg, beaten
25 mini empanada discs

Method of Preparation:
1. Cook the mushrooms over medium heat for about 10-15 minutes.
2. Add the raisins and balsamic vinegar.
3. Cook for 5 minutes more and. Let it cool down.
4. Take each mini empanada disc and put about half tbsp of mushroom filling and a bit of cheese in the center of each dough circle.
5. Seal it folding it in half and press the edge with a fork.
6. Brush each empanada with the beaten egg.
7. Preheat the oven to 400°
8. Bake for about 30 minutes.

QUINOA AND GOAT CHEESE EMPANADA

Sounds fancy, right? Well these empanadas are really easy to make. Quinoa is one of those super foods full of nutrients and benefits. Some of them: is full of protein, lots of fiber, iron and magnesium. Take advantage of all these benefits and make some healthy baked empanadas with quinoa.

Yields: 24 empanadas

Ingredients:
½ cup quinoa, dried
1 cup water
4 tbsp vegetable oil
1 red pepper, chopped
3 onions, chopped
3 eggs, boiled and chopped
10 oz. goat cheese, cubed
A pinch of salt
A pinch of black pepper
24 empanada discs

Method of Preparation:
1. In a pan, add quinoa and water; bring to boil and let it over medium heat until the quinoa absorbs all the water, let it cool down.
2. In a skillet, heat the oil and mix all the veggies and sauté for a couple of minutes.
3. Then, add the eggs and goat cheese into the quinoa.
4. Mix both fillings and let it rest before assembling the empanadas.
5. Take each empanada disc and fill it with a tbsp of the quinoa mixture.
6. Fold the disc in half and seal it with your fingers.
7. Preheat the oven to 375°
8. Bake the empanadas for about 25-30 minutes or until golden, don't over bake.

Green Plantain and Cheese Empanada

Green plantain empanada or how they call them in Ecuador "empanadas de verde". These are patties made with green plantain dough and filled with cheese. These empanadas are really popular as breakfast in Ecuador. You can also fill them with ground beef.

Yields: 10 empanadas

Ingredients:
6 green plantains, cooked
4 tbsp butter
½ cup water
A pinch of salt
2 cups white cheese
Vegetable oil, for frying

Method of Preparation:
1. Take the plantains and smash them the same way as preparing mashed potato.
2. Add the butter and mix it well.
3. Add the water and keep smashing until get dough with little crumbs of plantain.
4. Take a ball of dough and make it flat with your fingers.
5. Put some cheese inside and close it with another piece of dough.
6. In a pan, heat the vegetable oil and fry the empanadas until hard and golden.

PLANTAIN AND BLACK BEANS EMPANADA

Prepare these delicious, healthy and vegetarian empanadas and change your typical lunch for this amazing plate. If you want them to be extra yummy, prepare also a cheese dipping sauce or a garlic dipping sauce with a bit of hot sauce.

Yields: 6 empanadas

Ingredients:
1 tbsp olive oil
1 onion, chopped
1 cup black beans, cooked
1 clove garlic, minced
2 yellow plantain peeled and diced
2 tbsp cilantro, chopped

For the dough:
2 ½ cups all-purpose flour
A pinch of salt
½ tsp chili powder
4 tbsp butter
1/3 cup water
1 tbsp white wine vinegar

Method of Preparation:
1. To make dough, in a bowl, mix all the dry ingredients.
2. Make a hole in the middle of the dry ingredients and start adding the water, butter and vinegar.
3. Knead until get soft dough.
4. Wrap it in plastic and let it chill for at least 2 hours before using it.
5. For the filling, sauté the onions in a skillet over medium heat.

6. Add black beans and garlic; keep cooking for around 3-5 minutes more.
7. Add the yellow plantains; cook for 5 minutes more. Remove from heat and add the cilantro.
8. Take a part of the dough; roll it in a flat circle shape.
9. Put 2 tbsp of filling inside each dough circle.
10. Seal it folding it in half and press the edge with your fingers.
11. Preheat the oven to 400°
12. Bake the empanadas for about 25-30 minutes.

EGGS AND POTATO EMPANADA

Are you ready to make an ultra-tasty and healthy empanada? Well, this recipe is super easy and delicious. You can make it fried or baked, this time we are going to make them baked but choose the way you prefer. Serve these with a pink dipping sauce; tomato sauce, mayonnaise and some pepper.

Yields: 8 empanadas

Ingredients:
3 potatoes, diced
1 onion, diced
3 eggs, boiled and scrambled
2 tbsp olive oil
A pinch of salt
A pinch of pepper

For the dough:
2 ½ cup all-purpose flour
1 egg
½ cup butter
A pinch of salt
A pinch of pepper

Method of Preparation:
1. Heat the olive oil in a pan over medium heat, add the onion.
2. Add the diced potatoes and spices. Cook for about 3 minutes, stirring.
3. Finally, add the scrambled egg and seasoned it with salt and pepper.
4. For the dough, in a bowl, mix all the dry ingredients.
5. Beat a little bit the egg.
6. Make a hole in the middle of the dry ingredients.

7. Add the egg and butter.
8. Knead until get soft dough
9. Preheat the oven to 400°
10. Roll the dough and cut circle shapes. You can use a jumbo cookie cutter.
11. Put 1-2 tbsp of filling in the middle of the dough circles.
12. Close the circles in half and press the edges with a fork.
13. Bake for 30 minutes or until golden.

Eggplant Empanada

These vegetarian empanadas are made with a delectable marinara sauce and parmesan cheese. The eggplants are a great antioxidant, are full of vitamins, minerals and also help to lower the cholesterol.

Yields: 12 empanadas

Ingredients:
1/4 onion, chopped
2 cloves garlic, chopped
1 tbsp olive oil
A pinch of salt
A pinch of pepper
15 oz tomatoes, crushed
2 eggplants, cubed and roasted
8 oz parmesan cheese

For the dough:
3 cups all-purpose flour
6 oz butter, cold and cubed
1/4 tsp salt
1 egg
6 tbsp water

Method of Preparation:
1. In a large skillet, sauté all your ingredients, except tomato, for about 10 minutes.
2. After, add the tomatoes and stir for 5 minutes more.
3. Let it cool down.
4. For the dough, mix the dry ingredients and add the little butter cubes.

5. Smash the butter and start combining it with the flour.
6. Add the egg and water and mix until get soft dough.
7. Roll pieces of dough in a round shape.
8. Put some of the filling in the middle of each dough circle.
9. Seal the dough in half.
10. Preheat oven to 375°
11. Bake for around 30 minutes.

Sweet Empanadas

Chocolate filled with Dulce de Leche Empanada

It does not matter if you call it dulce de leche, cajeta, arequipe or manjar, I'm almost sure you like it and that you're going to love this recipe. It's a perfect dessert for any celebration or even just to have at home for your guests or children.

Yields: 24 empanadas

Ingredients:
32 oz dulce de leche
3 cups flour
¾ cup cocoa powder
½ cup sugar
Pinch of salt
8 oz butter, diced
2 eggs
6 tbsp water

Method of Preparation:
1. For the dough, mix all the dry ingredients.
2. Add the butter and combine with the other ingredients.
3. Add the eggs and water, mix until form dough.
4. Let the dough rest in the fridge for at least 15 minutes.
5. Take a part of the dough; roll it in a flat circle shape.
6. Put half a tbsp of dulce de leche inside each chocolate dough circle.
7. Seal it folding it in half and press the edge with your fingers.
8. Preheat the oven to 400°
9. Bake the empanadas for about 25 minutes.

Banana Empanada

These empanadas are perfect for dessert! Imagine a banana single pie, awesome, right? Serve with some chocolate syrup or even better, with ice cream and chocolate syrup.

Yields: 12 empanadas

Ingredients:
3 bananas, ripped
1 ½ cups flour
A pinch of salt
3 tbsp sugar
8 tbsp butter, diced
1 egg yolk, beaten
¼ cup water

Method of Preparation:
1. Take a large bowl, mix all the dry ingredients, add the butter and mix until get dough with little pieces of crumbs.
2. Add the egg yolk and keep mixing.
3. Add the water and knead a bit.
4. Let the dough rest for about 1 hour.
5. Preheat the oven to 400°
6. Roll the dough and cut circle shapes.
7. Put 1 tbsp of banana filling in the middle of the dough circles.
8. Close the circles in half and press the edges with a fork.
9. Bake for 20 minutes or until golden.

Apple and Cinnamon Empanada

These empanadas are like little apple pies. This empanada is perfect to serve at any celebration. Make them large for a great dessert or mini for little appetizers.

Yields: 30 mini empanadas

Ingredients:
2 tbsp butter
5 green apples
1/2 cup sugar
2 teaspoons cinnamon
¼ cup brown sugar

For the dough:
1 cup butter, chilled
8 oz cream cheese, chilled
2 1/3 cups flour
1 tbsp sugar
1 tsp salt
1 tsp vanilla

Method of Preparation:
1. Cut the apples in little cubes.
2. Put the apples in a pan; add sugar, brown sugar, butter and cinnamon.
3. Take off the heat and let it rest a bit.
4. For the dough, mix the dry ingredients and add the little butter cubes.
5. Start combining it with the flour.

6. Add the cream cheese and vanilla; mix until get soft dough.
7. Roll pieces of dough in a round shape.
8. Put some of the apple filling in the middle of each dough circle.
9. Seal the dough in half.
10. Preheat oven to 375°
11. Bake for around 30 minutes.

Strawberry and Raspberry Empanada

This is what I call a summer recipe. These empanadas are sweet, yummy, easy and healthy, what else do you need? Prepare these for breakfast or brunch with a freshly made orange juice.

Yields: 12 empanadas

Ingredients:
1 ½ cups strawberries, sliced
1 cup raspberries
1/3 cup sugar
12 empanada discs

Method of Preparation:
1. Put a pan over low heat and add strawberries and raspberries.
2. Add sugar.
3. Stir for around 4-5 minutes.
4. Preheat the oven to 400°
5. Take each empanada circle and put 1-2 tbsp of filling in the middle.
6. Close the circles in half and press the edges with a fork.
7. Bake for 25 minutes or until golden.

PINEAPPLE AND COCONUT EMPANADA

These pineapple and coconut empanadas are delicious. The coconuts are a really healthy fruit; speeds the metabolism, so it helps to prevent obesity. That's not the only benefit of this fruit; it also improves digestion, is gluten free, high in fiber and has antiviral healing properties.

Yields: 12 empanadas

Ingredients:
½ cup condensed milk
½ cup plain yogurt
1 cup pineapple, chopped
1 cup sweetened coconut, shredded
3 tbsp cornstarch
1/3 cup water
12 empanada discs

Method of Preparation:
1. In a saucepan, mix condensed milk and yogurt over low heat.
2. Add coconut and pineapple.
3. Start adding the cornstarch and water while stirring the mixture.
4. Mix for about 3 minutes. And then, let it cool down for 20 minutes.
5. Take each empanada disc and fill it with a tbsp of the pineapple and coconut mixture.
6. Fold the disc in half and seal it with your fingers.
7. Preheat the oven to 375°
8. Bake the empanadas for about 25 minutes or until golden, don't over bake.

S'MORES EMPANADA

These crunchy, sweet, chewy empanadas are just awesome. Do them for a campfire day or just to eat at home on a movie night! This is the perfect recipe to make for the celebration of the National S'mores Day on August 10th.

Yields: 6 empanadas

Ingredients:
6 large empanada discs
3 Hershey's chocolate candy bar
6 jumbo marshmallows
6 tbsp cookie butter

Method of Preparation:
1. Cut the chocolate candy bars in half; cut the jumbo marshmallows in two pieces also.
2. Put a piece of chocolate, two pieces of marshmallows and a tbsp of cookie butter inside each empanada disc.
3. Seal it folding it in half and press the edge with your fingers.
4. Preheat the oven to 400°
5. Bake the empanadas for about 25 minutes.

Banana and Nutella Empanada

This is a really famous combination. You can find cakes, cupcakes, ice cream, cookies, pies, crepes and more with these two ingredients. But the thing is that this mix is perfect! So now, it's time to make banana and Nutella empanadas to delight everyone.

Yields: 8 empanadas

Ingredients:
2 cups flour
½ tsp salt
10 tbsp butter, cubed
1/3 cup water
1 banana, cubed
1 cup Nutella
2 tbsp sugar

Method of Preparation:
1. For the dough, mix the dry ingredients and add the little butter cubes.
2. Start combining it with the flour.
3. Add the cream cheese and vanilla; mix until get soft dough.
4. Roll pieces of dough in a round shape.
5. Put some of the banana in the middle and add a tbsp of Nutella over the bananas of each dough circle.
6. Seal the dough in half.
7. Preheat oven to 375°
8. Bake for around 20 minutes.

BLUEBERRY AND CHOCOLATE EMPANADA

What about a delicious blueberry chocolate little empanada? These empanadas are perfect for a tea party or to eat with coffee. Blueberries are low in calories, are a great source of vitamin A, vitamin C, calcium and iron.

Yields: 30 mini empanadas

Ingredients:
1 lb blueberries, frozen
3/4 cup sugar
2 cups dark chocolate chips

For the dough:
4 cups flour
½ cup sugar
½ tsp salt
1 tsp baking powder
1¼ cups butter
½ cup water

Method of Preparation:
1. In a pan over low heat, add the blueberries and sugar, star stirring.
2. After about 20 minutes, take it off the heat and let it cool down.
3. For the dough, mix the dry ingredients and add the little butter cubes.
4. Mix everything well.
5. Roll pieces of dough in a round shape.
6. Put some of the blueberry filling in the middle of each dough circle and add some chocolate chips on over the blueberries.
7. Seal the dough in half, pressing the edges with your fingers.
8. Preheat oven to 375°
9. Bake for around 20 minutes.

STRAWBERRY AND CREAM CHEESE EMPANADA

Strawberries and cream cheese is just a soft and lovely combination. This looks like an empanada for a princess. Make them with fresh jumbo strawberries.

Yields: 10 empanadas

Ingredients:
8 oz cream cheese, room temperature
1/3 cup sugar
3 egg yolks, room temperature
1 tsp vanilla extract
¼ tsp salt
1 tbsp lemon zest
2 cup fresh strawberries, diced
10 empanada discs

Method of Preparation:
1. Take the strawberries and cream cheese in a bowl, cream them.
2. Then add the vanilla, egg yolks, salt and lemon zest, keep creaming until smooth.
3. Pour a tbsp of strawberry filling inside each empanada disc.
4. Seal it folding it in half and press the edge with your fingers.
5. Preheat the oven to 375°
6. Bake the empanadas for about 15-20 minutes.

Apricot and Cream Cheese Empanada

This is a summer empanada, perfect for a pool day. These are soft, sweet, crunchy, and perfect! Use real apricots for an extra. Don't forget that you can always change the fruits depending on what you have at home.

Yields: 25 empanadas

Ingredients:
3 apricots, chopped
2 tbsp sugar
½ cup cream cheese, room temperature
A pinch of salt
½ tbsp lemon zest
½ tbsp vanilla
1 pack pie crust mix

Method of Preparation:
1. In a pot, add 1 tbsp sugar and apricots, boil for about 10 minutes. Remove and let it cool down.
2. In a bowl, add cream cheese, the other tbsp of sugar, salt, lemon zest and vanilla. Whisk all the mixture.
3. Add the apricots to the cream cheese mix. Stir until combine.
4. Take the pie crust mix and roll it over a table.
5. Cut little circles with a big cookie cutter, or a glass.
6. Put half tbsp of filling inside each dough circle.
7. Seal it folding it in half and press the edge with your fingers.
8. Preheat the oven to 350°
9. Bake the empanadas for about 20 minutes.

APRICOT, BANANA AND RICOTTA EMPANADA

This is another recipe of empanadas with fruits. This time you're going to add ricotta to this delightful combination. Apricots and bananas are both soft and sweet fruits. Serve these with vanilla ice cream on the side.

Yields: 40 mini empanadas

Ingredients:
5 large bananas, diced
1 cup ricotta
½ cup apricot jam

For the dough:
3 cups flour
½ tsp salt
1 ½ stick butter, chilled
5 tbsp water

Method of Preparation:
1. For the dough, take a bowl, mix all the dry ingredients, add the butter and combine well.
2. Add the water and knead until get soft dough
3. Let the dough rest for about 20 minutes.
4. For the filling, take another bowl and combine bananas, jam and ricotta.
5. Divide the dough in 40 little balls.
6. Take each ball and make a flat round shape.
7. Add about half tbsp of the filling in the middle.
8. Seal the dough folding it in half and pressing the edges with a fork.
9. Preheat the oven to 350°
10. Bake for about 20 minutes.

Nutella and Strawberry Empanada

What can I say about the sweet, delicious, chocolaty Nutella? Well, I can say that is the main ingredient for this recipe. This is a quick and yummy option for any dessert.

Yields: 6 empanadas

Ingredients:
4 large strawberries
6 tbsp Nutella
6 empanada discs

Method of Preparation:
1. Slice each strawberry in three slices.
2. Take each empanada disc and fill it with a tbsp of Nutella and 2 pieces of strawberry.
3. Seal it folding it in half and then press the edges with your fingers.
4. Preheat the oven to 400°
5. Bake the empanadas for 15 minutes.

51705081R00052

Made in the USA
San Bernardino, CA
29 July 2017